BEST 25 PLACES TO VISIT IN
PARIS

1. Notre Dame Cathedral

One of Paris' most enduring symbols: Notre-Dame de Paris, also known as Notre Dame, is a Roman Catholic cathedral on the Ile de la Cité's eastern part. It is widely regarded as one of France's and Europe's greatest examples of French Gothic architecture. With its entrances surrounded by his many sculptures and gargoyles that grace the ceiling, this cathedral, begun in 1163 and completed in 1345, is a marvel to behold.

We recommend taking a tour of the cathedral before entering and climbing the 387 steps to the summit of the towers. The journey to the top of the towers is strenuous, but it rewards you with a panoramic view of the region and close-up views of the iconic gargoyles.

Memories

Date:

2. Louvre Museum

The Louvre is the world's most visited art museum. This ancient edifice, a former royal palace, is located in the heart of Paris and has a total area of 210,000 square meters, including 60,600 square meters for exhibitions. The museum is housed in the Louvre, which was once a fortress built by Philip II in the late 12th century. The remnants of the stronghold may be seen in the museum's basement.

There are eight sections to the collection:

- Sculptures of the Middle Ages, Renaissance and Modern Times
- Objects of art
- Paintings
- Graphic arts.
- Egyptian antiquities
- Oriental antiquities
- Greek, Etruscan and Roman
- Islamic Art

Memories

Date:

3. Champs Elysées / Arc of Triumph

Napoleon commissioned Jean Chalgrin to construct a triumphal arch dedicated to the glories of imperial soldiers, under the spell of ancient Roman architecture. It is the world's largest monument of its sort, having been built in the nineteenth century. Its pillars are adorned with stunning sculptures. The names of 558 generals, as well as major triumphs, are inscribed on the arc's summit. The Tomb of the Unknown Soldier of France is located beneath the Arc de Triomphe.

A wonderful view of Paris may be had from the panoramic terrace over the door. The Arc de Triomphe stands 50 meters tall, 45 meters wide, and 22 meters deep on the Place de l'Etoile, which leads to the Champs Elysees, dubbed "the most beautiful boulevard in the world."Between the Place de la Concorde and the Arc de Triomphe, it spans 1.9 kilometers. There are numerous high-end retailers (Louis Vuitton, Cartier, Guerlain, Montblanc, etc.), entertainment venues (Lido, theaters), and well-known cafes and restaurants (Fouquet's).

Memories

Date:

4. Eiffel Tower

What would Paris be like if it didn't have its iconic Eiffel Tower? It was built by Gustave Eiffel to commemorate the French Revolution's centennial and was unveiled during the Exposition Universelle in Paris in 1889. With approximately 7 million tourists every year, it is one of the most visited sites in the world, standing 324 meters tall.

The Eiffel Tower 58, which spans two storeys and stands 58 meters above ground, is located on the first floor. The view from the second level is the greatest at 115 meters, with a diving view of the earth below. Finally, on the 3rd level, at a height of 275 meters, you can view what Gustave Eiffel's office looked like. It is possible to use the stairs and ascend the steps for the more daring (1,665 to the summit).

The climb to the top of the Eiffel Tower is a must-do if you want to get a spectacular perspective of Paris.

Memories

Date:

5. Montmartre

Montmartre is a 130-meter-high hill in Paris's northwestern outskirts that gives its name to the neighboring district. The white-domed Basilica of the Sacred Heart, located at the summit, is its most famous feature. It was finished in 1919 and is dedicated to the French victims of the Franco-Prussian War of 1870.

If you're in the area, stop by the Tertre Square, which is just a few blocks away from the Basilica. Many artists have set up their easels to paint tourists or to display their work. The Place du Tertre is a reminder of the early twentieth-century period when Montmartre was the epicenter of contemporary art, with painters such as Amedeo Modigliani, Claude Monet, Pablo Picasso, and Vincent van Gogh working there. A few feet from the Square of Tertre is the Espace Salvador Dal, a museum dedicated mostly to the Spanish painter's sculpture and drawings.

Montmartre is home to the world-famous cabaret Moulin Rouge.

Memories

Date:

6. Palace of Versailles

The Château de Versailles is France's most well-known chateau. Versailles was the center of political power in the Kingdom of France from 1682 until 1789. It was built in the 17th century as a symbol of French military prowess and a demonstration of French supremacy in Europe. This massive complex of buildings, gardens, and terraces is a must-see for any visitor who will be enchanted by the luxurious accommodations, opulent furnishings, furniture, and gilded Renaissance pieces of art.

The State Apartments and the famed Hall of Mirrors, the Queen's chamber, are the first stops on your tour of Versailles. Don't miss a stroll around the well-known "French" gardens.

Memories

Date:

7. The Latin Quarter - Luxembourg park

The Sorbonne is located on the left side of the Seine, in the Latin Quarter of Paris. The Latin Quarter is home to various higher education institutions, including the Ecole Normale Superieure, the Ecole des Mines de Paris, and the Ecole Polytechnique. It is known for its student life, lively ambiance, and bistros. The Latin language, which was previously widely spoken at and around the University because Latin was the international language of study in the Middle Ages, inspired the area's name.

The Luxembourg Park is a public garden that was established in 1612 at Marie de Medicis' request to accompany the Luxembourg Palace. It is lovingly referred to as the "Luco" by Parisians. The Palais du Luxembourg, where the Senate sits, is surrounded by a garden. It has been redesigned by André Le Nôtre and is extremely pleasant to wander around; there is also an orchard, various species of apples, an apiary, and an orchid collection in the greenhouse. There are 106 statues, including a bronze replica of the Statue of Liberty, as well as three lovely fountains.

Memories

Date:

8. Moulin Rouge

The Moulin Rouge is a cabaret that is credited as being the spiritual home of the famed French Cancan. It was created in 1889 by Joseph Oller and Charles Zidler in the middle of Pigalle, at the foot of Montmartre hill. The cancan, which began as a courting dance, gave rise to the cabaret, which is today found in many nations throughout the world. The Moulin Rouge is now a tourist attraction that entertains visitors from all over the world.

Its style and moniker have been copied and adopted by various nightclubs all around the world, including Las Vegas. In addition, various films, like as Baz Luhrmann's 2001 blockbuster starring Nicole Kidman and Ewan McGregor, have enhanced the cabaret's renown.

Memories

Date:

9. Musée d'Orsay

The Musée d'Orsay, located on the Left Bank in a former railway station, is known for its extensive collection of impressionist paintings. Paintings by French artists such as Degas, Monet, Cezanne, and Van Gogh, among many others, are on display. A number of sculptures, as well as photography and furniture, are on display in the museum. Through the museum's huge transparent clock, you can get a stunning view of the Sacré-Coeur Basilica if you ascend to the museum's top balcony.

Although the vast Louvre may appear to receive the most of the attention in Paris, recent visitors appear to prefer the Musée d'Orsay. Travelers say the museum is far more bearable than the sometimes overpowering Louvre, and that there are far fewer crowds here. Many tourists confidently claim that this museum can be easily navigated in a few hours. Travelers praised both the museum's vibrant collection of paintings and the structure itself, with many hailing the d'Orsay's Belle Epoque architecture as a work of art in and of itself.

Memories

Date:

10. Musee de l'Orangerie

The Musée de l'Orangerie, a branch of the Musée d'Orsay, houses a large collection of impressionist and post-impressionist paintings. It is most renowned for Claude Monet's enlarged "Water Lilies" paintings. The eight colossal paintings are divided into two oval rooms with a glass canopy that floods the space with natural light. These paintings were enlarged by Monet in order to thoroughly immerse spectators in their beauty, especially after the difficulties of World War I. Aside from the "Water Lilies" series, the Jean Walter-Paul Guillaume collection at the Musée de l'Orangerie includes works by Renoir, Cézanne, Picasso, Matisse, and others.

This gallery is a must-see for museum visitors, especially Monet enthusiasts. They were relieved to learn that it was a pretty tiny structure, which means it can be built quickly if you're in a hurry. The smaller area also means there are fewer people in the museum, which many visitors liked.

Memories

Date:

11. Pere-Lachaise Cemetery

Is it possible to make a tourist attraction out of a cemetery? If there's one city that can do it, it's Paris. The Père-Lachaise Cemetery, which spans about 110 acres in the 20th arrondissement (district), is regarded as one of the most beautiful cemeteries in the world. It is also the largest green space in Paris. Père-Lachaise is a network of cobblestone roads lined with lush, cascading trees that provide the perfect shade for the grounds' magnificent 19th century burial chambers. Père-Lachaise is one of the most famous burial grounds in the world, with everyone from Oscar Wilde and Jim Morrison to Edith Piaf and Gertrude Stein interred there. However, before you go, pick up a map because there are 70,000 burial places here.

Memories

Date:

12. Palais Garnier

   The Opéra Garnier, also known as the Palais Garnier, is a masterwork of architectural luxury that still emits the same enigmatic mood it did in the late 1800s. The opera's palpable feeling of intrigue and mystery is owed in part to the Garnier's awe-inspiring Old World interiors, as well as Gaston Leroux, the author of "Phantom of the Opera," which was inspired by the Garnier. The ghost was alleged to be genuine by Leroux, who successfully incorporated real-life opera events (such as the chandelier falling and killing a bystander) into his fiction. Many people have wondered if there was a dweller beneath the opera because of the Garnier's lack of a strong historical record and Leroux's literary abilities. Staff have stated otherwise, but it's easy to see how the idea could be so plausible, especially given the opera's very genuine underground lake. Leroux's story might never have come to fulfillment if it hadn't been for Napoleon III, who commissioned the opera.

Memories

Date:

13. Luxembourg Gardens

 The Luxembourg Gardens are a warm-weather haven that offers the simplest of joys, with plenty of green space (61 acres) for sunbathing and people-watching, as well as plenty of activities to keep kids entertained. When the hustle and bustle of the city becomes too much, take a stroll around the walks and formal gardens, or simply relax with a picnic. At the Grand Basin, kids can float sailboats, ride ponies, ride the merry-go-round, or watch a puppet performance at the on-site Theatre des Marionettes. Adults will enjoy the on-site Musee du Luxembourg, which was the first public museum in France. The Luxembourg Gardens, with 106 sculptures, including a replica of the Statue of Liberty, may easily be regarded an open-air museum in and of itself.

Memories

Date:

14. Musée Rodin

The Musée Rodin is a hidden gem in the city, as it is the former home of famous 19th-century sculptor Auguste Rodin. Rodin's expressive sculptures, such as The Hand of God, The Kiss, and The Thinker, among others, have taken the place of furniture and tacky lawn ornaments. Aside from the sculptures, there are 7,000 sketches by the artist on exhibit, as well as a section dedicated to his muse and mistress, artist Camile Claudel. Visitors will also be able to see works from Rodin's personal art collection, which includes Van Gogh paintings.

Recent visitors considered Rodin's sculptures to be nothing short of breathtaking, and they highly recommend a visit even if you aren't an art connoisseur. The stunning on-site gardens were another great hit, and for some visitors were just as important as the art. The grounds, along with the museum's manageable size, generated a quiet and peaceful ambiance not often encountered in other prominent Parisian museums, according to visitors.

Memories

Date:

15. Centre Pompidou

The Centre Pompidou is one of Paris' most popular cultural destinations. But keep in mind – as previous visitors have confirmed – that if you're not a fan of modern art, you're unlikely to like this museum. The Pompidou is a museum dedicated to modern and contemporary art (think cubist, surrealist and pop art, among others). Even the building's façade is a little "out there," with its interiors (piping, plumbing, elevators, escalators, and so on) visible from the street.

One of the world's largest collections of modern and contemporary art may be found inside the inside-out museum (more than 100,000 pieces of art). The National Museum of Modern Art of France, which houses works by 20th and 21st-century artists, is the most prominent attraction within. Big names like Matisse, Picasso, and even Andy Warhol can be found here. Additional exhibition and entertainment venues, as well as a library, rooftop café, and cinemas, are all located within the Centre Pompidou.

Memories

Date:

16. Paris Catacombs

Not every inch of Paris is as romantic as you might imagine - the Catacombs, in particular, are eerily unsettling. Prior to the late-eighteenth-century construction of the Catacombs, Parisians buried their dead in cemeteries. However, as the city grew, burial sites ran out of room, and tombs became exposed, stinking up the neighboring neighborhoods. The solution was eventually found in the limestone quarries 65 feet beneath Paris, which provided adequate and safe space for the city's deceased loved ones. It took 12 years to relocate 6 million remains from Parisian cemeteries.

The melancholy, skull-and-bone-lined tunnels that weave beneath the heart of the City of Love today lure visitors with an interest in the dead. The catacombs spread for miles around the city, but visitors are only permitted to see a mile of them for 45 minutes at the Denfert-Rochereau metro station (lines 4,6 and RER B). Attempting to enter the catacombs using any other entrance in the city is prohibited. Because the paths inside are gravelly, uneven, and even slippery in places, you'll want to wear sturdy footwear. Expect a line because to the attraction's unique character and popularity.

Memories

Date:

17. PLACE

"Il y a tout ce que vous voulez aux Champs-Élysées," as singer Joe Dassin once sung, translates to "There's everything you could want along the Champs-Élysées." And he is correct. The Arc de Triomphe is a shopper's paradise, running more than a mile from the gleaming obelisk at Place de la Concorde to the foot of the Arc de Triomphe. Luxury businesses like Louis Vuitton and Hugo Boss rub shoulders with less-expensive establishments like Adidas and Gap along its spacious, tree-lined sidewalks.

While the Champs-Élysées is undeniably a shopping heaven, recent visitors have noted that most store prices can be quite exorbitant. And the more cheap ones are frequently overcrowded. The Champs-Élysées are no exception. Because this is such a well-known boulevard in Paris, expect to see throngs of people both during the day and at night. Nonetheless, many visitors liked soaking in the lively atmosphere of the Champs-Élysées and seeing locals and tourists come and go.

Memories

Date:

18. Sainte-Chapelle

The stained glass windows at Sainte-Chapelle are unrivaled in Paris. The 1,113 episodes from the Old and New Testaments of the Bible are depicted in vibrant color on the panes, which date back to the chapel's construction in the 13th century. Sainte-Chapelle is a treasured example of French Gothic architecture that originally housed Christian items collected by Louis IX. It was built in under seven years. Between 2008 and 2014, the structure had a thorough repair and is now open to the public every day of the year save Christmas Day, New Year's Day, and May 1 (France's Labor Day). For those aged 25 and up, admission costs 10 euros (about $11) per person, with free tickets available for EU residents. Guided tours take 45 minutes and are available between 11 a.m. and 3 p.m. For an extra 3 euros (about $3) per participant, audio tours are offered.

Memories

Date:

19. Seine River

   The Seine runs right through the centre of Paris, so you won't have any trouble finding it. The river is one of the most well-known waterways in the world, and it is a tourist destination in and of itself. It serves a functional purpose as well: it flows from east to west, dividing the city into the Left and Right Banks. Knowing where you are in respect to the Seine will assist you in navigating the city throughout your visit.

   The river is usually used as a photo background for visitors, yet it provides a lifeline for people. It's a steady source of water, a significant transit corridor, and a vital conduit for a variety of trade. Since the 3rd century, it has also been a source of nourishment for many fishermen. The Seine River was designated as a UNESCO World Heritage Site in 1991 due to its historical and contemporary cultural value.

Memories

Date:

20. Galeries Lafayette Paris Haussmann

  The Galeries Lafayette Paris Haussmann department store is a sight to behold, whether or not you intend to shop. What began as a modest curiosity shop in 1893 has since expanded to a 750,000-square-foot megastore with hundreds of brands ranging from affordable selections like Levi's and Nike to high-end labels like Prada and Cartier. And, when you're enthralled by the never-ending array of stylish items, don't forget to gaze up. The spectacular neo-Byzantine glass dome, which rises 141 feet above the ground, is the luxury bazaar's showpiece. On the top floor of the skyscraper, there's also a glass walkway that allows the boldest of visitors to stand over all the excitement below.

  Several recent visitors have dubbed Galeries Lafayette the world's most beautiful shopping center, pointing out that the majestic structure is a destination in and of itself, even if you aren't shopping for expensive goods. They also recommend visiting the complex's roof, which is open to guests for free and offers amazing views of the city below.

Memories

Date:

21. Louis Vuitton Foundation

The Louis Vuitton Foundation, which has been open to the public since October 2014, is the brainchild of the LVMH group (which owns luxury fashion brand Louis Vuitton) and renowned American architect Frank Gehry. Gehry also created the Guggenheim Museum in Bilbao, Spain, and the Walt Disney Concert Hall in Los Angeles, among other prestigious museums, academic buildings, and residences. The Foundation's audacious and futuristic design stands out among Paris' plethora of centuries-old structures, with curving glass panels and smooth concrete. Inside, you'll find permanent and temporary displays with collections of modern and contemporary art. The museum's mission is to promote art and culture on the outskirts of Paris, and it accomplishes this purpose by attracting over 1 million visitors each year. Visitors appreciated taking in the architectural wonder and its surrounding gardens, as well as the interesting displays within, despite the museum's location in the 16th arrondissement being a bit off the main road. They suggested purchasing a ticket in advance to avoid the huge waits. The building was criticized for being too far from the nearest metro station (approximately a 15-minute walk), so keep that in mind when planning your visit.

Memories

Date:

22. Conciergerie

The Conciergerie, located near to Sainte-Chapelle, was originally a royal home for numerous French leaders. King Charles V and the rest of the palace's inhabitants relocated to the Louvre at the end of the 14th century. The abandoned structure was eventually converted into the kingdom's new parliament and office space. The Conciergerie, on the other hand, served as a prison compound for both political and common offenders throughout the French Revolution (and for many decades afterward). It was most famous for housing Marie Antoinette, France's fallen queen, in the weeks leading up to her guillotine execution in October 1793. Antoinette's cell was converted into a chapel in the nineteenth century, and the entire edifice was declared a historic monument and opened to the public in 1914.

Visitors can pay between 7 and 9 euros ($8 to $10) per person to enter the site. Recent visitors stated the site is a treat for history aficionados, especially if they read the informative inscriptions and view the instructive videos located around the structure. Others suggested that if you aren't very interested in the French Revolution or Marie Antoinette, the empty jail cells and dreary halls can be a little boring. The medieval building, which is reported to be gorgeous both inside and out, was something that everyone seemed to agree on.

Memories

Date:

23. Pantheon

The Panthéon, a massive church and burial ground in Paris' Latin Quarter (or 5th arrondissement), has a long and illustrious history. During its early years, the structure served as a mausoleum, a church, and an art museum, and it was completed in 1789, at the onset of the French Revolution. To show the rotation of the Earth, scientist Leon Foucault constructed the Foucault pendulum within the building in 1851. The pendulum was removed and replaced several times before being replaced with a copy in 1995, which is still in use today. Voltaire, Jean-Jacques Rousseau, and Marie Curie are among the many renowned historians, philosophers, scientists, and writers buried in the Panthéon's crypt.

The museum's notable gravesites and Foucault's pendulum were popular with recent visitors. They also suggested taking a dome tour for spectacular views of Paris; from the top, you'll be able to see the Eiffel Tower, as well as many other well-known landmarks. Nonetheless, several people complained that the admission charge was excessive.

Memories

Date:

24. Jardin des Tuileries

  The Jardin des Tuileries is a 55-acre free public garden in the heart of Paris, between the Louvre and the Place de la Concorde. The park was included to the UNESCO World Heritage list in 1991 (as part of the Banks of the Seine) and has been available to the public since the 17th century, despite being created mainly for the benefit of the royal family and court. Green space has played a significant part in the history of France. Foreign dignitaries once convened in the Jardin des Tuileries for meetings, and Napoleon and Marie-wedding Louise's procession marched through the gardens on its way to the couple's now-defunct Palais des Tuileries wedding supper.
  Parisians and tourists alike enjoy strolling around the park's tree-lined walks, enjoying picnics on the lawn, or simply people-watching from a bench. The park is a terrific location to unwind on the route to or from the Louvre, according to recent visitors. The Musée de l'Orangerie, located at the southwest end of the grounds, is also nearby. There are three restaurants, a bookstore, a carousel, and other attractions in the gardens.

Memories

Date:

25. Le Marais

Le Marais is one of Paris' oldest and coolest districts, straddling the 3ème and 4ème arrondissements (districts). It's so hip, in fact, that French novelist Victor Hugo (author of "The Hunchback of Notre Dame" and "Les Misérables") named it home. It's easy to imagine yourself strolling through medieval Paris, with its cobblestone alleys, imposing stone structures, and tucked-away courtyards. Le Marais was once home to some important French royalty. The creation of the Place des Vosges, Paris' oldest square, was overseen by King Henry IV. For a time, Louis XIV called this neighborhood home before deciding to relocate his family and court to Versailles. Much of Le Marais was also spared during the French Revolutionary War.

Memories

Date:

www.ingramcontent.com/pod-product-compliance
Lightning Source LLC
Chambersburg PA
CBHW040424100526
44589CB00022B/2820